D0461005

000604

Anthony Quinn 604

Life in the
THIRTEEN COLONIES

Rhode Island

Robin S. Doak

children's press®
An imprint of
SCHOLASTIC

Library of Congress Cataloging-in-Publication Data

Doak, Robin S. (Robin Santos), 1963–
  Rhode Island / by Robin S. Doak.
    p. cm. — (Life in the thirteen colonies)
  Includes bibliographical references and index.
  ISBN 0–516–24578–3
  1. Rhode Island—History—Colonial period, ca. 1600–1775—Juvenile literature. 2. Rhode Island—
History—Revolution, 1775–1783—Juvenile literature. I. Title. II. Series.
  F82.D63 2004
  974.5'02—dc22

                    2004001941

A Creative Media Applications Production
Design: Fabia Wargin Design
Production: Alan Barnett, Inc.
Editor: Laura Walsh
Copy Editor: Laurie Lieb
Proofreader: Tania Bissell
Content Research: Lauren Thogersen
Photo Researcher: Annette Cyr
Content Consultant: David Silverman, Ph.D.

CONTENTS

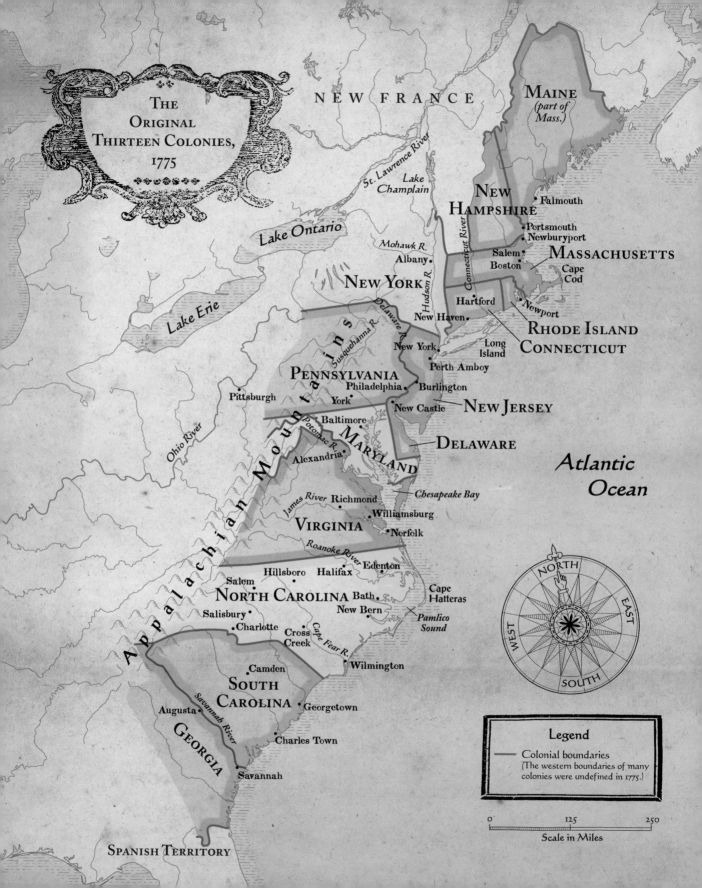

THE
ORIGINAL
THIRTEEN COLONIES,
1775

NEW FRANCE

MAINE
(part of Mass.)

St. Lawrence River

Lake Champlain

NEW HAMPSHIRE

Falmouth

Portsmouth
Newburyport

Lake Ontario

Mohawk R.

Albany

NEW YORK

Connecticut River

Salem
Boston

MASSACHUSETTS

Cape Cod

Lake Erie

Hudson R.

Hartford

Newport

New Haven

RHODE ISLAND
CONNECTICUT

Delaware R.

Susquehanna R.

New York

Long Island

Perth Amboy

Appalachian Mountains

PENNSYLVANIA

Philadelphia

Burlington

NEW JERSEY

Pittsburgh

York

New Castle

Ohio River

Baltimore

Potomac R.

MARYLAND

DELAWARE

Alexandria

Atlantic Ocean

James River

Richmond

Chesapeake Bay

Williamsburg

VIRGINIA

Norfolk

Roanoke River

Edenton

Hillsboro

Halifax

Salem

NORTH CAROLINA

Bath

Cape Hatteras

Salisbury

New Bern

Charlotte

Cross Creek

Cape Fear R.

Pamlico Sound

Camden

Wilmington

SOUTH CAROLINA

Georgetown

NORTH

Augusta

Savannah River

EAST

WEST

GEORGIA

Charles Town

SOUTH

Savannah

Legend

Colonial boundaries
(The western boundaries of many colonies were undefined in 1775.)

0   125   250

Scale in Miles

SPANISH TERRITORY

A Nation Grows
From Thirteen Colonies

Rhode Island is located in the northeastern part of the United States in the region called New England. It is bordered by Massachusetts on the north and east and by Connecticut on the west. Its southern border is formed by the Atlantic Ocean.

Rhode Island's native people lived along the shores of the Atlantic Ocean and Narragansett Bay. They also lived among the wooded hills of western Rhode Island. The first European settlers came to find a place to practice their religion freely.

The colony established one of the most democratic governments among the thirteen colonies. Rhode Islanders were known for their independent spirit. Although it was the smallest colony, Rhode Island contributed mightily to the formation of the new nation.

The map shows the thirteen English colonies in 1775. The colored sections show the areas that were settled at that time.

CHAPTER ONE
Discovery

The Europeans Arrive

On a stormy April day in 1524, Italian explorer Giovanni da Verrazano guided his ship, *La Dauphine,* into a small bay along the coast of what is now Rhode Island. From the shore, groups of native people watched in amazement as the big vessel approached. They had never seen a ship like this one. Verrazano, in turn, watched the people on land. He did not know if they would be friendly. He did not know if they would attack the ship and chase him from their territory.

The natives waved and shouted greetings. Some even paddled out to the ship in canoes to meet the newcomers. The ship's crew welcomed the natives aboard. The crew offered them gifts of bells, glasses, and other trinkets. For the next two weeks, Verrazano and his crew were treated to the hospitality of Rhode Island's native people.

Giovanni da Verrazano astonished the native people when his large sailing ship landed in Newport harbor.

European Exploration

In the early 1500s, people in Europe knew little about North America. This mysterious land sparked their imaginations. Some Europeans thought that a waterway across North America might connect Europe to the spice-rich lands of Asia. King Francis I of France decided that his country would be the first to find this shortcut.

Like other monarchs, Francis wanted to control the valuable trade of silk and other riches with China. In 1523, King Francis hired Verrazano to explore North America in search of the route to Asia that would become known as the Northwest Passage.

Verrazano set sail from France in January 1524. His ship, *La Dauphine,* was 60 feet (18 meters) long, about the size of a modern tractor-trailer truck. The ship carried a crew of fifty men. In March, Verrazano made landfall along the coast of North Carolina, then began sailing northward. He explored the Atlantic coast, sailing into New York Harbor before arriving in what is now Narragansett Bay in Rhode Island. There, he was warmly greeted by native peoples of the area, probably members of the Narragansett or Wampanoag tribes.

Verrazano liked the natives he met in the region that would become Rhode Island. He wrote a letter to the king of France describing the region's native people. In the letter,

Verrazano described the natives as having long black hair, black eyes, and "brass-colored" skin. They wore deerskins. "This is the goodliest people and of the fairest conditions that wee have found in this our voyage," the explorer told Francis.

Verrazano was also impressed by the land he had found. In the letter to King Francis, the explorer described it as "pleasant as is possible to declare very apt for any kinde of husbandry of corn, wine, and oyle." He talked about the fertile lands, clear rivers, and thick woods filled with wildlife. Verrazano named the area "Luisa," after the king's mother.

Verrazano never did find a shortcut to China. The French were not interested in the land he had found.

How Rhode Island Got Its Name

In a letter to the king of France, explorer Giovanni da Verrazano compared an island off the coast of what is now Rhode Island to an island in the Mediterranean Sea called Rhodes. Some people believe that this letter is where Rhode Island's name came from. Others think that the name was given to the region by Dutch explorer Adriaen Block, who called it *Roodt Eyland,* or "red island," because of its red clay shores.

By 1643, a few settlements had been established in the area. The settlers obtained a **charter** from Great Britain, which made their settlements an official colony. Under this charter, the colony was called the Providence Plantations. Twenty years later, the colony got a new charter and a new name: Rhode Island and the Providence Plantations. Today, this is still the state's official name.

In 1614, Dutch explorer Adriaen Block ventured into the area. Block wanted to trade with the Indians for furs to sell in Europe. He was the first European to see the riches of the Rhode Island area. He established two short-lived trading posts and discovered an island, which he named Block Island, after himself.

Native Peoples of Rhode Island

Long before European explorers set foot on Rhode Island, other people made their homes in the region. Nearly 8,000 years before Verrazano sailed along the coastline, the ancestors of Indian tribes lived there. The earliest Indians were **nomads** who hunted and gathered nuts and plants to survive.

At the time Verrazano explored the area, five main Native American tribes lived in Rhode Island. These tribes were the Narragansett, Niantic, Nipmuc, Pequot, and Wampanoag. The largest and most powerful tribe in the region was the Narragansett. Historians believe that the group numbered about 7,000 in the early 1600s.

The Narragansett were frequently at war with other area tribes. They fought often with the Wampanoag, as well as with the Pequot in Connecticut and the Mohawk in New York. The Narragansett also brought many of the smaller tribes in the area under their control. This meant that the small tribes had to pay tribute, or send gifts, to the Narragansett.

Around the year 1616, an **epidemic** of disease, brought to the area by European explorers and fishers, caused the deaths of hundreds of Wampanoag. The native people had no natural defenses against European diseases, so they were at high risk for serious illnesses. Some historians believe that as many as 75 percent of the Wampanoag died during the epidemic.

Entire Wampanoag villages were wiped out by smallpox brought to Rhode Island by Europeans.

The epidemic left the Wampanoag and many other tribes throughout the area seriously weakened so they could not fight off their enemies. The Wampanoag's enemies, the Narragansett, were unaffected by the epidemic. As a result, the Narragansett were even more powerful after the epidemic was over.

The Narragansett

The Narragansett tribe lived around the shores and on the islands of Narragansett Bay. Tribal life was centered around the villages. The Narragansett had eight major villages. Each village had its own chief, called a **sachem.** The largest village was located near what is now Kingston, Rhode Island. It had two sachems who ruled over the rest of the village leaders. People in the Narragansett villages were usually related to each other.

Work in a Narragansett village was divided by gender. Women farmed, planting corn, pumpkins, squash, and beans. They prepared animal skins for clothing and other uses, collected berries and roots to eat, and watched the children. The women also set up the **wigwams** that tribal families lived in. The word *wigwam* was not an Indian word. It was made up by colonists. It was their way of simplifying the native word *wetuomuck*, which means "at home."

The Narragansett wigwam was most often square or rectangular with a rounded top. The outside was covered with grass mats and tree bark that were sewn together to form shingles. In the center of the roof, a hole allowed

Narragansett wigwams were rectangular structures with rounded roofs. Wigwams were clustered together to form villages.

smoke from a cooking fire to escape. The Narragansett women sometimes decorated the inside of their homes with colorful embroidered hangings called *munnotaubana*.

The men in a Narragansett village hunted and fished. In the forests, they caught deer, moose, raccoon, beavers, squirrels, and turkeys. For fishing in the cold waters of the Atlantic Ocean, the men made canoes out of tree trunks. First they burned the trunks. Then they dug out the charred wood to create a hollowed-out space. The Narragansett were also skilled net makers and made bone hooks and spears to catch their prey, which included bluefish, sea bass, trout, herring, and eels. They dug oysters, clams, and mussels out of the tidal shores.

Narragansett men also grew tobacco. The natives believed that this plant cured headaches and arthritis. The men often wore a bag of tobacco and a pipe around their neck. They also used roots, herbs, and tree bark to treat fevers, eye problems, wounds, and other conditions.

Another native method of staying healthy was the sweat bath. The sweat bath was a small hut plastered with mud to make it airtight. Water was poured on top of heated stones inside the hut to create hot steam. After sweating in the heat for a while, the natives took a cool dip in a nearby river or lake.

In the summer, the tribe lived near the ocean where the weather was pleasant. As the weather turned colder, they moved inland, away from the frigid ocean breezes.

Narragansett Fun and Games

The Narragansett and other tribes of the Rhode Island area were hardworking, but they also loved to have a good time. They enjoyed games, music, and dancing. Roger Williams, an Englishman who would later settle in the area, described the tribes' love of one particular game: "They have great meetings of foot-ball playing, onely in Summer, towne against towne, upon some broad sandy shoare, free from stones, or upon some soft heathie plot because of their naked feet, at which they have great stakings, but seldome quarrell." During "foot-ball" matches, teams tried to kick a ball, made of deerskin and filled with moss, through goalposts set about a mile apart. Williams said that hundreds of people flocked to the games to cheer for their team.

The Narragansett participated in many types of contests, including canoe races. They often placed bets with each other on the outcome.

The winners would receive furs and other prizes.

Other games tested skill and speed. The Indians participated in tomahawk throwing, archery contests, and foot and horse races. They also enjoyed gambling with stones, bones, and sticks, which were tossed in the same way people today toss dice.

During the winter, the tribe ate corn that had been ground into cornmeal in the summer and stored. The cornmeal was used to make cakes that were later called johnnycakes by the Europeans. The Narragansett also ate dried berries, nuts, and roots.

Early Contact

The first Europeans to have an impact on the native peoples were the Dutch traders of the early 1600s. Dutch traders were mostly based in New York and Connecticut. They wanted the furs of beavers and other animals that roamed the area in order to sell them in Europe. Since the Indians were expert hunters, the Dutch left it to them to do the hunting. The Dutch, in turn, would trade for the furs. The Dutch thus introduced Rhode Island's Indians to the idea of buying and selling goods.

The Dutch used Indian wampum to buy furs. Wampum was strings of dark purple and white beads made out of seashells that had been drilled and polished. The word *wampum* comes from a Narragansett word meaning "white shell bead."A number of Atlantic coast tribes, including the Narragansett, made wampum. The Narragansett were known throughout the region for their skill at making wampum. During the summer, men of the Narragansett and other tribes gathered shells at the beach. In the winter, they fashioned tube-shaped beads that could be left loose or strung together on sinew (an animal tendon used as a cord). The strands of beads were worn around the neck and on the wrists.

Wampum was highly prized by Rhode Island tribes. The strings of beads showed a person's social status. The beads were worn only by the most important tribal members. Sachems and others wore wampum woven into aprons, hats, belts, and moccasins. Women wore wampum as earrings, bracelets, and in headdresses.

Wampum was also used by the tribes in ceremonies and for many other purposes, including paying tribute to stronger tribes and paying ransom for captives. The Dutch quickly learned that natives of the area were willing to trade furs for these strands of shells. Wampum was thus used sometimes as money is used today.

Wampum Woes

Like money today, the value of wampum rose and fell depending upon the market. When the Narragansett acquired metal drill bits from the Europeans, the making of wampum became much easier. Since it was now easy to make, there was soon a lot of it. Too much wampum in the market meant that the shell beads were not as valuable as they once were.

Another problem was counterfeit, or fake, wampum. Some dishonest European traders made black wampum beads out of stones, bones, and glass. As a result, the Massachusetts Bay Colony made strict rules about the quality of wampum that could be used as "money."

The Effects of Trade

As trade between the native people of the Rhode Island area and the Europeans increased, the native people started to depend upon the Europeans for some of the items they needed. For instance, the Europeans gave the Indians metal arrowheads and knife blades. These replaced the stone weapons the Indians had used for centuries. The Indians did

Native Americans brought beaver pelts to trade with white settlers. In return, they received metal tools, pots, and sometimes guns and gunpowder.

not have the technology to make metal weapons and tools themselves, so they depended on trade with the Europeans to get them.

To acquire European goods, the Indians needed furs to trade. Some tribes began using more of their time to trap animals for their fur. They spent less time hunting and fishing. Traditional customs, crafts, and even diets began to change as the natives came to rely on trade with the Europeans. Native languages were also affected as Indians began using English words.

Although early contact with European explorers and traders affected the native people, greater change was soon to come. More than a hundred years after Giovanni da Verrazano sailed into Narragansett Bay, the region would be settled by English people from the nearby Massachusetts Bay Colony. The native people would soon have to share their lands with the English newcomers.

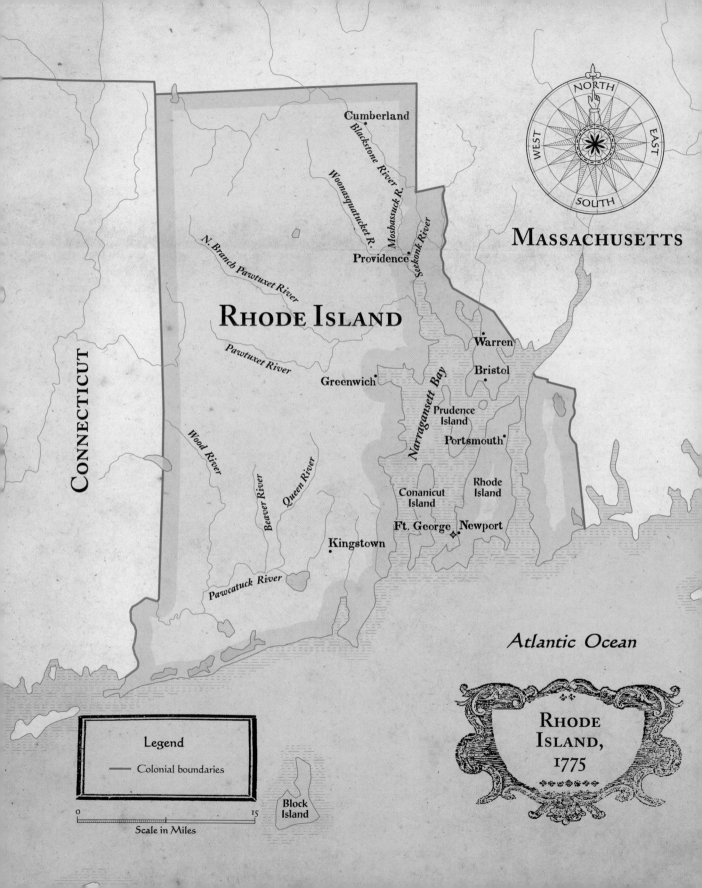

CUMBERLAND

Blackstone River

Woonasquatucket R.

Mosbassuck R.

N. Branch Pawtuxet River

Seekonk River

PROVIDENCE

RHODE ISLAND

Pawtuxet River

WARREN

BRISTOL

GREENWICH

Narragansett Bay

Prudence
Island

PORTSMOUTH

Wood River

Beaver River

Queen River

Conanicut
Island

Rhode
Island

Ft. George • NEWPORT

KINGSTOWN

Pawcatuck River

CONNECTICUT

MASSACHUSETTS

NORTH
EAST
SOUTH
WEST

Atlantic Ocean

Legend

— Colonial boundaries

Block
Island

0   15
Scale in Miles

RHODE
ISLAND,
1775

CHAPTER TWO

A Place of Refuge

The First Settlers

The first European to settle in Rhode Island was an English preacher named Roger Williams. In January 1636, Williams fled to Rhode Island from the Massachusetts Bay Colony. The preacher had been banished from Massachusetts for openly disagreeing with the colony's Puritan leaders. In Rhode Island, Williams took shelter with the Wampanoag at their winter camp in what is now Warren.

In the spring, Williams was joined by several supporters. They built houses on the eastern shore of the Seekonk River in Rhode Island. But since that area was also under the control of the Massachusetts colony, Williams was not allowed to stay there. Officials from Plymouth sent a letter to Williams telling him to move off their territory right away.

This map shows how Rhode Island looked in 1775.

Roger Williams

Englishman Roger Williams arrived in Massachusetts in 1631. His open-minded views about religion quickly got him in trouble with Puritan leaders in the colony. Williams was also more sympathetic than most settlers to the native people of the area. He believed that the English king had no right to give English settlers land in Massachusetts that belonged to native tribes.

In the early 1630s, Williams wrote these thoughts in a manuscript. The Massachusetts leaders worried that Williams's words would influence others. In 1633, Massachusetts leaders forced him to burn the manuscript.

In 1635, Massachusetts officials put Williams on trial for his beliefs. He was found guilty. When Williams learned that the Puritans were going to ship him back to England, he escaped to Rhode Island.

Roger Williams found refuge with Native Americans after being cast out from Massachusetts.

A Place Called Providence

Williams then crossed to the other side of the Seekonk. This land, on the western side of the river, was controlled by the Narragansett tribe. Two Narragansett sachems gave Williams a large piece of land. To thank them, Williams gave the natives many gifts.

Soon, twelve families joined Williams. Together, they built the first permanent settlement in Rhode Island. Williams named the little colony Providence, in honor of the care he felt that God had given him when Williams fled Massachusetts. (*Providence* means the guidance or care of God.) The settlement was founded on the idea that Providence would be a safe place for anyone who wanted to live there.

After settling in Rhode Island, Williams continued to treat the natives of the area fairly. "Nature knows no difference between European and American [Indian] in blood, birth, bodies, etc.," he wrote. Throughout Williams's life, he worked hard to keep peace between the colonists and the regional tribes. In 1645, he even helped Massachusetts officials make peace with the Narragansett.

Williams traded with the native tribes. He also preached to them about Christianity. However, Williams never forced his beliefs on tribal members. The preacher also learned the language, Algonquian, that was spoken by both the

Narragansett and Wampanoag. He later wrote a book called *A Key into the Language of America*. Today, the book gives readers a valuable glimpse into the lifestyle of Rhode Island's Indians.

Williams was honest when he dealt with the native people. As a result, he had the trust and friendship of the Narragansett and Wampanoag throughout his life. The fact that the Native Americans liked and respected Roger Williams was also good for Rhode Island's first colonists.

The New Settlement

In 1637, the original thirteen families to settle in Providence made up an agreement about how the town should be governed. The heads of each family signed a document called the "town fellowship." By signing, each family promised to show "active or passive obedience to all such orders as shall be made for the public good." That meant they agreed to follow the rules of the settlement. These rules were about the government of the settlement only. When it came to religion, the people of Providence were free to worship as they pleased.

Providence, like later Rhode Island towns, had a "town meeting" form of government. At these meetings, citizens had the chance to speak out and vote on issues that affected them. At a town meeting in 1721, for example, the men of Providence decided to do something about gray squirrels in town. Squirrels were pests and their population was booming. The men voted to pay people two pence (about two cents) for every gray squirrel head they presented to the town treasurer. All of the squirrels had to be killed in Providence.

In 1636, Roger Williams landed at this spring and founded the town of Providence, Rhode Island.

In 1640, townsfolk created a five-member board of governors, known as the Disposers. The Disposers were in charge of the town's general business. They also acted as mediators when disagreements arose between townspeople. The Disposers had to listen to any Providence resident who

Roger Williams's cabin was the first house to be built in Providence. Other log and timber homes were soon built by his followers.

wanted to speak at a town meeting. The Disposers also were not allowed to interfere with any person's choice of religion.

With a system of law and order in place, the settlement began to grow slowly. In 1640, Providence's population numbered about a hundred people. These early settlers had to clear the land, dig wells for water, and build homes. The very first houses were shelters dug into the sides of hills. Later, the settlers built log cabins with dirt floors and **thatched** roofs made of grass and straw. The cabins were built close to each other and were later connected by a road.

As carpenters and stone masons came to the colony, larger houses were built. These houses were built like farmers' homes in England. They usually had two stories. The lower story was called a fire-room, and the small upper story was for sleeping. The central feature of the house was a huge fireplace in the fire-room that was used for cooking and heating. The houses were usually made of heavy timbers covered with boards and shingled roofs. Since there was no glass in the colony at first, windows were covered with paper or cloth soaked in oil to let light in and keep the rain, snow, and cold out.

Homes in Providence were usually small and plain, both inside and out. Most early families had little furniture. A typical colonial Providence home had chairs or benches, chests for storage, and bedrolls called "shake-downs" that could be rolled up during the day. For a table, settlers propped up a long wooden board. As many as a dozen people might share one house.

Roger Williams's home was the first to be built in Providence. He built it on a spot where two rivers met. Williams's house was larger than other houses in town because Williams planned to use it as a Sunday meeting-house as well.

Farming and Eating in Providence

During the settlement's earliest days, Williams's friendship with the Narragansett paid off. When the settlers did not have enough food, the tribe offered them gifts of corn and turkeys. Williams also traded with the tribe to get food and other supplies to help the settlers through the first years. Wampum was used as money between the two groups. Dark beads were worth twice as much as white beads.

The Narragansett helped the settlers in other ways. They taught the newcomers how to plant corn, beans, and squash in the same mound of earth. Corn was planted at the top, with the beans underneath. The corn grew first, and then the beans used the cornstalks as a pole to grow on. The big leaves of the squash plants stopped weeds from growing. A fish placed in each mound made good fertilizer, helping the vegetables grow. The Narragansett also helped the settlers with other tasks, including fence building.

Providence's men, women, and children worked hard to make the settlement a decent place to live. Each family had an area behind the home for gardens and orchards. In addition to corn, beans, and squash, settlers grew fruits, grains, and pumpkins.

Men and boys picked fruit at the family orchard. Everyone worked hard to make sure there was enough food for all.

The Rhode Island Clambake

The native peoples of Rhode Island taught the settlers how to make a clambake. A clambake is a way of cooking clams in the sand of a beach. A large hole was dug in the sand. Clams were baked in the hole using hot rocks and seaweed. Clam chowder and cornmeal johnnycakes were also served at the event. The clambake became a popular event for early colonists. Some historians believe that the discovery of huge middens, or piles of clamshells, shows that the Narragansett and other native peoples enjoyed the clambake tradition long before the colonists arrived.

In the 1800s, Rhode Island clambakes became popular with tourists who visited the state. Today, visitors can still enjoy a traditional clambake on the Rhode Island shore.

Later, they would grow potatoes and tobacco, for their own use and for sale. Even young family members helped with farming and other chores. Children were expected to feed the chickens, weed the gardens, and help make soap or candles.

At first, settlers spent most of their time fishing and hunting. They caught eels, mackerel, and shellfish to add variety to their diets. In the forests, they hunted for deer and smaller game. Later, the colonists kept livestock such as cows, chickens, sheep, and pigs, which they slaughtered for meat. A large open field in the center of town served as a grazing area for the townspeople's livestock.

Business in Providence

Soon other businesses and trades were started in Providence. In 1640, the settlement's first gristmill was built. A gristmill is a mill for grinding grains into a powder called meal. The meal is then used in recipes to make breads and cereals.

Gristmills were powered by waterwheels. The force of the water from a stream or river turned the waterwheel, which moved large grinding stones inside the mill.

Anne Hutchinson

Anne Hutchinson, a Puritan, came to the Massachusetts Bay Colony from England in 1634. Her husband, William, and their fourteen children traveled with her.

Soon after arriving in Massachusetts, Anne Hutchinson became unhappy with the colony's Puritan leaders. She began holding meetings in her home to talk about politics and religion. Many of Hutchinson's first followers were women. But she attracted a number of male followers as well, including some ministers and colonial officials.

Hutchinson's meetings also made her some important enemies. Puritan officials worried that the outspoken leader was stirring up

Anne Hutchinson was tried by a court in Massachusetts before she was banished.

trouble and setting a bad example for other colonial women. In 1637, Massachusetts Bay officials banished Hutchinson from their colony. Governor John Winthrop called her "a woman not fit for our society."

Later, a **tannery,** a place where animal skins were turned into leather, was built. A tavern, jail, and animal pound were also added to the town.

Women worked in the home. They cooked and preserved food, washed and sewed clothing, and taught the children. Women also worked in the fields. They helped plow, plant, and pick the family's food crops. Since everyone was needed to pitch in and help the family survive, most colonial women also knew how to do such tasks as slaughter animals and perform basic carpentry work.

The wives of millers, tanners, and other tradesmen often worked as partners in the family business. Some kept track of the money, while others worked side by side with their husbands in blacksmithing, shoemaking, and other trades. Many colonial women had their own home businesses. These businesses ranged from drying and selling herbs used as medicines to sewing and embroidering.

To sell their goods or visit their neighbors, Rhode Island colonists used the many rivers and waterways around Providence. Soon after Providence was founded, a ferry system was started so people could cross the Moshassuck River. Other ferries soon followed. Later, bridges were built to span the waterways. The bridges replaced the ferries. They made it easier for people to get from one place to another.

Riding Shank's Mare

During early colonial days, most Rhode Islanders got from one place to another on foot. Walking became known as "riding shank's mare." The shank is the part of the leg between the knee and the ankle. A mare is a female horse. Wealthier citizens did not have to ride shank's mare. They usually traveled on horseback, on a regular mare.

Searching for Religious Freedom

It was not long before word of Roger Williams's settlement spread to other colonies. Since citizens of Providence were allowed to practice any religion they pleased, the settlement attracted other religious outcasts. Like Roger Williams, many of the settlers came from the Massachusetts Bay Colony, where the Puritans' laws against those who disagreed with them were severe. The first people to join Williams and his supporters were Anne Hutchinson and more than eighty of her supporters. Like Williams, Hutchinson had been banished from Massachusetts because of her religious beliefs.

Roger Williams was happy to help the new settlers. He asked the Narragansett to give some land on Aquidneck Island (a small island in Narragansett Bay) to Hutchinson and the others as a favor to him. In return, Hutchinson gave the Narragansett "forty fathoms [240 feet] of white beads [wampum]," along with some coats and hoes. In 1638, Hutchinson, her husband, William, and William Coddington founded the settlement of Portsmouth on Aquidneck Island. By 1642, two new towns, Newport and Warwick, had been added to the growing colony.

The four original towns of Rhode Island (Providence, Portsmouth, Newport, and Warwick) operated independently. The groups that had founded each town were very different from each other in their views of religion and the law. Each town wanted to make up its own rules.

In 1640, however, Portsmouth and Newport decided to join together and share one government. William Coddington was the first governor of thc town. This government didn't last. The two towns soon split and resumed their own governments.

Rhode Island accepted people of differing religious beliefs. Small churches such as this one were built throughout the colony.

It would be many decades before the Rhode Island settlements joined together to become a single colony. In the colonies that surrounded Rhode Island, the people had their Puritan religious beliefs in common. Rhode Island, with its religious freedom, did not have a single religion to unite its settlers.

Troublemakers

Sometimes Rhode Island's well-known tolerance attracted troublemakers and lawbreakers who had been forced out of other colonies. The colony soon had a reputation as a place of "chaos" and "depravity." Other colonies looked down on the Providence settlement and the freedom its citizens had. In the words of Governor John Winthrop of Massachusetts, "At Providence…the devil was not idle."

Other colonies tried to isolate and punish Rhode Island for its freethinking ways. In 1643, the colonies of Massachusetts, Plymouth, Connecticut, and New Haven formed a confederation, or group, known as the United Colonies of New England. (In 1665, New Haven would join the Connecticut colony; in 1691, Plymouth would become part of the Massachusetts colony.) The confederation was created to protect the member colonies from common enemies. It also hoped to someday stop Roger Williams's settlement. When the Rhode Island settlements asked to be admitted to the group, the confederation said no—unless the Rhode Island settlements agreed to be controlled by either Massachusetts or Plymouth. Rhode Island colonists refused. People in Rhode Island did not want to take orders from any other colony.

Even though it was not part of the United Colonies of New England, Rhode Island continued to grow. Williams and his fellow colonists were determined to make their settlement a success, with or without the help of their neighbors. In the coming years, they would prove that they could survive and prosper.

A Bostonian's View of Rhode Island

In a 1695 book, Puritan minister Cotton Mather, from Boston, described Rhode Island. His views were shared by many people in nearby colonies. Mather wrote, "I believe there never was held such a variety of religions together on so small a spot of ground as have been in that colony....So that if a man had lost his religion, he might find it at the general muster of opinionists." In other words, Mather and others believed that people who went to Rhode Island could pick and choose any religion they wished. In Mather's opinion, this was not the correct way to practice religion at all.

CHAPTER THREE

The Providence Plantations

Banding Together

In the mid-1600s, Rhode Island faced serious threats from nearby colonies. Beginning in 1642, both Connecticut and Massachusetts began to claim land that had been given to Roger Williams and other settlers by the Narragansett. Both colonies believed that the Rhode Island settlers had no legal claim to the land. Connecticut and Massachusetts also thought that the Rhode Island settlers were under their control and should obey their rules.

Williams and other colonists realized that they needed to protect themselves from their neighbors. Williams proposed that the four fiercely independent settlements of Rhode Island should band together to protect their lands

ᕗ *Roger Williams and his men return from England with the Rhode Island charter, creating the Providence Plantations.*

and freedom. Williams also offered to travel to Great Britain and talk to the king. He hoped to convince the king to grant Rhode Island a royal charter. The royal charter would make Rhode Island an official English colony, separate and independent from other English colonies.

In the summer of 1643, Williams set off for Great Britain. He returned to Rhode Island later that year with a royal charter in hand. The charter declared that Providence, Portsmouth, and Newport were now a single colony, officially named the Providence Plantations. Warwick was later included in the charter. The surrounding area was still known as Rhode Island, as it had been since the days of the earliest European exploration.

The charter was different from other colonial charters. While most charters required that a certain religious system be set up in the new colony, the charter of the Providence Plantations did not mention religion at all. In addition, the charter allowed people in the colony to elect their own leaders.

Rhode Island had always attracted people who had been persecuted, or punished, because of their beliefs. With the new charter, it attracted even more. Persecuted people from other American colonies as well as England and other nations came to the Providence Plantations. They all wanted a place where they could live and pray as they wished.

Religious Freedom

In 1658, groups of Jewish settlers began arriving in Newport. In 1763, the Jewish community there finished building Touro Synagogue. This was the first Jewish house of worship in America. By 1739, the colony was home to more than thirty places of worship, including Congregationalist, Baptist, Anglican (Episcopalian), and **Quaker** churches.

Touro Synagogue, as it looks today, was dedicated in December 1763. From 1781 to 1784, Rhode Island's General Assembly met here.

Quakers were one of the most persecuted religious groups in the colonies. Also known as the Society of Friends, the Quakers followed their own special set of rules and customs. For example, they would not take off their hats in court, and they were opposed to war for any reason. They also used old-fashioned, formal language that made them seem even more different from others. As a result, the Quakers were harassed and laws were passed against them. They were forced to practice their religion in secret. In Massachusetts, Quakers were even hanged for their beliefs.

Beginning in 1650, many Quakers fled to Rhode Island. By 1700, more than half of Newport's population was Quaker. William Coddington, the settlement's founder, became a Quaker later in his life. Quakers were important to the political, economic, and social life of Newport.

Early Government

In May 1647, the Providence Plantations formed a General Assembly. This was a government in which all four towns were equally represented. The General Assembly's first meeting was held in Portsmouth. At the meeting, officials talked about the freedom of government that had been granted in their charter: "The form of Government established in Providence Plantations is Democratical, that is to say, a government held by the free and voluntary consent of all."

At the first meeting, ten colonial officers were elected. The leading officer was known as the president. The first president was John Coggeshall of Newport. Roger Williams, William Coddington, and two others were named as his assistants. In 1654, Roger Williams was elected the colony's president. He held the position for three years.

Women played an important role in Quaker religious services, unlike in many other religious groups.

Rhode Island as an English Colony

Providence and the other Rhode Island towns grew and flourished. By 1655, Rhode Island's population had grown to about 1,200 people.

At first, the most important source of income for the colony was farming. Fertile land allowed farmers to grow good crops of corn, hay, and tobacco. Extra crops were

Rhode Island's settlers loaded extra crops onto sailing ships to trade with other colonies for goods they needed.

traded with other colonies and with Great Britain. Livestock, including cattle, horses, and hogs, was also raised and sold by Rhode Island farmers. Animal furs, which had been one of the earliest sources of money, were no longer important to the colony. Other colonies, such as New York and Pennsylvania, now dominated the fur trade.

In 1650, Great Britain passed the first of a number of laws that became known as the **Navigation Acts**. These laws were created mainly to protect British trade. However, the Navigation Acts hurt Rhode Island's economy. They put limits on the types of goods that colonists could make and sell. English businesses did not want colonial goods competing with their own goods.

Not all Rhode Island colonists obeyed the new laws. Some continued to make goods that were banned by law. Others were willing to smuggle these goods into and out of Narragansett Bay.

Great Britain also banned the printing of paper money and the making of coins in the colonies. As a result, cash was hard to find in Rhode Island. Instead, colonists used the barter system. In this system, they exchanged their extra crops for the tools and other products they needed. The lack of cash affected Rhode Island's colonial government. When it was time for residents to pay taxes, they often paid the government with goods instead of money. But the government needed money to operate.

Despite the ban on printing money, Rhode Island made its own paper money between 1710 and 1750. The money was supposed to be used for tax payments to the colonial government only. Instead, the paper money began circulating throughout Rhode Island and other colonies. People started to use it for payment for goods and services.

While colonial officials dealt with the many problems caused by Great Britain, colonial settlers faced challenges of their own. Every day, Rhode Island families struggled to survive and thrive in their new homes. Each family member, children included, had to pitch in and help.

Growing Up in Rhode Island

For the very youngest Rhode Islanders, survival itself could be a struggle. Many colonial children died as babies. Others died before reaching adulthood. They were killed by diseases such as smallpox, measles, and pneumonia. During the 1600s, as many as 40 percent of all children in the region now known as New England (Rhode Island, Connecticut, Massachusetts, Vermont, New Hampshire, and Maine) died before reaching adulthood.

As in other colonies, much of a Rhode Island child's life was spent working. From the age of three, boys and girls were expected to do chores. What little time was left after work was used for learning to read and other basic skills.

Children's Clothing

Colonial toddlers, both boys and girls, wore full-length, long-sleeved dresses made out of linen or wool. They were made in many colors, including black, gray, blue, green, red, purple, and yellow. The dresses were laced in the back and had high necklines. Underneath, young boys and girls wore a long underdress, usually made of linen. Around the age of six, boys were "breeched," or put into short pants called breeches.

As they grew, both boys and girls would begin to dress more like their parents. For a girl, this might mean wearing a petticoat (a type of skirt), lace collar, and hooded cloak (similar to a cape). Girls also began wearing stays, which were tight, close-fitting undergarments with strips of bone or wood to make them stiff. The stays, worn around the chest,

This well-dressed boy is wearing a lace collar, doublet, knee-pants, and stockings.

were thought to help girls stand straight. A boy might begin wearing a doublet (a type of jacket), waistcoat (vest), and lace collar and ruff (a pleated collar). Under all this, he wore a plain linen shirt.

During the early colonial days, Rhode Island boys and girls were taught at home. Boys learned how to read and add and subtract numbers. They also learned the trade, such as blacksmithing or shoemaking, that they would practice when they grew up. Some girls also learned to read. This was usually done by sewing samplers, which were pieces of cloth with letters and numbers embroidered, or stitched, into them. Later, girls read the Bible and other books to improve their skills.

The first public school in the colony was started in Newport in 1640, but it didn't last long. The schoolmaster soon left the colony and the school was closed. Schools were started in other towns, but education was not required by law in the colony. By 1672, every colony except Rhode Island had laws that said that all children were required to go to school. In fact, it would be more than 125 years before such laws were passed in Rhode Island in 1800.

In the middle 1700s, "dame schools" were popular in Providence and Newport. Dame schools for girls and boys were run by housewives or widows in their own homes. In these schools, students learned reading, writing, and spelling, as well as French and music. Some schools taught dancing. Even so, most colonists felt that learning from books was not considered important for girls. They felt it was more important that girls learn skills that would be useful around the house, such as embroidery and sewing.

Around the age of fourteen, boys were often apprenticed to local tradesmen to learn a trade. As apprentices, boys learned skills that would help them prosper and contribute to the colony as adults. Boys worked side by side with adult tradesmen, called masters, to learn a trade. If the apprentices hadn't already learned mathematics and reading, their masters would teach them enough so that they could handle money and read the Bible.

Like the young colony they lived in, colonial children in Rhode Island had much to learn. Although the future looked promising, there were many challenges ahead.

Fun and Games in Colonial Rhode Island

Despite all the work and schooling, colonial kids still found ways to have fun. Rhode Island children played some of the same games that children still enjoy today, including tag and hopscotch. Other pastimes included spinning tops, blowing soap bubbles, shooting marbles, and flying kites. In the winter, Rhode Island children enjoyed sledding and skating. As the new colony grew and prospered, there would be less work for children and more time for fun.

CHAPTER FOUR

A Thriving Colony

New Threats

Even though it now had a charter and was an official English colony, Rhode Island was still being threatened by Massachusetts and Connecticut. In 1659, Massachusetts sent a group to buy Indian land in areas that Rhode Island claimed as its own. Then, in 1662, Connecticut received a new royal charter from Great Britain. This charter stated that all land up to the western shore of Narragansett Bay belonged to Connecticut. Rhode Island officials knew that their neighbor's new charter would wipe out their little colony. Only Newport and Portsmouth would remain independent, since these towns lay to the east of Narragansett Bay.

In 1663, King Charles II of England was persuaded by some Rhode Island leaders to grant a new charter to the colony. Along with the new charter, the colony received a

Trade with the Narragansett and other Indian tribes was an important part of Rhode Island's economy.

new name: Rhode Island and the Providence Plantations. The new charter forced Massachusetts to give up its claim to Rhode Island's land. This charter also made new boundaries between the colony and Connecticut. Connecticut's charter of 1662 was no longer a threat.

With the new charter, Rhode Island also became one of the few colonies allowed to elect its own governor.

The new governor of Rhode Island met with the deputy governor and twenty assistant governors.

(Governors in most of the other colonies were chosen by the king or other officials.) The new title of governor replaced the old one of president. There would also be elections for a deputy governor (like a vice president) and twenty assistants. Six of the assistants would be from  Newport and four each from Providence, Portsmouth, and Warwick. The last two assistants would be from future Rhode Island towns.

The charter was a victory against the United Colonies of New England, the group that had tried to exclude and punish Rhode Island for its independence. The charter said it was against the law for other colonies to threaten Rhode Island. This meant that Massachusetts and Connecticut could no longer harass and arrest anyone outside their own borders.

The charter also made Newport the colony's chief city. The government's main offices were located in Newport, and most of the early governors came from the town. The charter itself was first read to the public in Newport. It was kept there in a special case and taken out once each year when the colony's newly elected officials took their seats in the General Assembly.

Rhode Island colonists were very proud of the charter of 1663. In the coming years, they would fiercely defend the charter. They would fight those who would try to take it away. The charter would shape Rhode Island's government until 1843.

Troubles With the Indians

For most of Rhode Island's early history, colonists had a good relationship with the native tribes of the area. The colony treated the Narragansett and other tribes much more fairly than most other colonies treated native people. In 1673, for example, Rhode Island was the first colony in the region to allow Native Americans to sit on juries along with colonists when a case involved other Native Americans. The sachems of the Indians on trial were allowed to choose the native jurors who would decide whether those on trial were guilty of a crime.

Unlike settlers living in nearby colonies, Rhode Island colonists didn't try to force the Narragansett and other tribes to become Christians. In 1674, a Puritan named Daniel Gookin complained that none of the native peoples of Rhode Island had converted to Christianity. Gookin blamed this on Rhode Island's settlers. He wrote that, in Rhode

Island, "civil government and religion…runs very low." To him, it seemed that religion was not very important to Rhode Island settlers. Many other Puritans agreed with Gookin's opinion of Rhode Island and its settlers.

In general, Rhode Island colonists got along well with the Indians. This tradition started with Roger Williams's first meeting with Rhode Island's Native Americans.

King Philip's War

Although relations between Rhode Islanders and Native Americans were fairly good, trouble had been brewing in other colonies for many years. As more people settled in Connecticut and Massachusetts, the tribes in these areas were forced to sell more and more of their land. For some tribes, such as the Wampanoag, the Europeans had brought epidemic and death. In most cases, Native Americans had come to distrust Europeans.

In 1675, a Wampanoag leader named Metacomet (called King Philip by the colonists) brought together tribes throughout the areas surrounding Rhode Island. Metacomet wanted to get back land in the Massachusetts Bay Colony that had been taken from his people. He knew that if the tribes joined together, they would have a better chance of doing this. The tribes began attacking settlements in Connecticut and Massachusetts. This conflict became known as King Philip's War.

During the conflict, native warriors destroyed crops, burned towns, and killed colonists. Of the ninety settlements in the area, fifty-two were attacked and as many as thirteen were almost completely destroyed. Massachusetts settlements were hit especially hard.

When Indians raided settlers' farms during King Philip's War, they sometimes captured women and children rather than killing them. The captives were often released after a ransom was paid.

At first, settlers and native peoples in Rhode Island tried not to take sides. The Narragansett, for example, refused Metacomet's request to join his fight. William Coddington, Rhode Island's governor, even talked to Metacomet to try and stop the fighting. Despite these efforts, the Narragansett and Rhode Island colonists would soon be right in the middle of the violence.

On December 19, 1675, armed men from the United Colonies of New England attacked some Narragansett people near what is now South Kingstown, Rhode Island. The colonists killed 700 Indians, including about 400 women and children. The Great Swamp Fight, as the slaughter in Rhode Island became known, convinced the other Narragansett that they had to join the fight. They joined forces with Metacomet and his warriors.

In March 1676, the Narragansett attacked and burned Providence. Roger Williams tried to convince the warriors to leave in peace, but he failed. The Narragansett leader of the attack promised, however, not to kill Williams. "Brother Williams, you are a good man," he said. "Not a hair of your head shall be touched." Most of the settlement's buildings, including Williams's home, were destroyed. The town of Warwick was also attacked and nearly destroyed.

King Philip's War came to an end in August 1676, when Metacomet was killed. The war was the bloodiest in colonial history. Thousands of Native Americans and about 600 colonists died. After the war, the colonists took revenge on the tribes who had fought them. Many natives were executed. Many others were sold as slaves and sent to Caribbean islands. Very few Native Americans were left in the region.

*The death of Wampanoag chief Metacomet brought King Philip's War
to an end.*

Business Booms

After the violence and bloodshed of King Philip's War, Rhode Island colonists went back to building their colony. By the end of the 1600s, Rhode Island was a thriving colony, with several towns and more than 6,000 colonists. New towns included Westerly, Kingstown, and Jamestown.

The colony's economy had shifted from farming to ship-building, trade, and other activities that made the most of Rhode Island's coastal location. Businesses that depended on the ocean were set up in many towns. These businesses included shipbuilding and chandlery, or candle making. Rhode Island's chandlers were famous for making candles out of spermaceti, a waxy substance found in the heads of sperm whales. Rhode Island tradesmen were also known for their excellent iron and silver goods.

Newport was both the political and economic center of the colony. In fact, the town was one of the most important seaports in all of the colonies. It had 150 wharves (places where ships could dock) and hundreds of shops. From Newport, corn, furs, livestock, fish, lumber, and wool were shipped to Great Britain and the islands of the West Indies in the Caribbean, as well as to the other American colonies. Other important industries in Newport were shipbuilding and whaling, or fishing for whales for their oil and spermaceti.

Some Newport businesses, however, added to Rhode Island's bad reputation among other colonies. One of these was smuggling. Smugglers wanted to avoid paying the tax required by the Navigation Acts on certain goods being imported into the colony. The smugglers sneaked, or smuggled, these goods into Newport and other Rhode Island towns. They also smuggled goods out of the colony and into foreign ports that were forbidden by the Navigation Acts. Smuggling became even more common in the mid-1700s, when Great Britain called for more taxes and restrictions on goods.

Whaling was a dangerous occupation. Many sailors from Rhode Island lost their lives hunting the giant mammals.

Privateers and Pirates

Another business that added to Newport's bad reputation was privateering. **Privateers** owned ships that were hired by the colonial government to capture and rob enemy ships. Enemy ships were any vessels owned by nations at war with Great Britain. Privateering started during a series of conflicts that took place in the colonies between France and Great Britain from 1698 to 1763. During these wars, Great Britain hired private ships to attack the enemy's ships.

Newport was a good place for privateering. Many privateers from Massachusetts moved to Rhode Island. By the early 1700s, Newport was the colonies' privateering capital. From 1754 to 1763, fifty privateers operated out of the town. Although privateers were paid well by the government, privateering was a dangerous job. Between 1754 and 1763, about a hundred Newport sailors who tried to capture French ships were taken prisoner by the French.

There was not much difference between a pirate and a privateer. The main difference was that privateers were hired by the government to raid enemy ships. Privateering was legal. Pirates, on the other hand, worked for themselves, raided any ship they could, and broke the law.

Some people crossed the line between privateering and piracy. During times of peace, some greedy privateers raided ships throughout the Atlantic and Caribbean. Piracy was a problem because no ship was safe, even during peacetime. Although Great Britain demanded that Rhode Island put a stop to pirates whose ships had come out of Newport, the colony did little about piracy.

In 1699, Lord Bellomont, the royal governor of New York, Massachusetts, and New Hampshire, accused Rhode Island of "conniving at pirates and making Rhode Island their sanctuary." He criticized the colony for protecting pirates. At the time of Bellomont's death in 1701, he was working to have Rhode Island's charter taken away because of the piracy problem. This did not happen, but Bellomont did convince Rhode Island to do something about pirates. In 1723, twenty-six pirates were hanged in Newport.

When pirates captured a ship, everyone in the crew shared in the loot.

One famous privateer-turned-pirate who had ties with Rhode Island was William Kidd. Kidd used Conanicut Island in Narragansett Bay as a hideout, and Rhode Island merchants paid for some of his voyages. When Kidd was arrested and hanged in London, some of his Rhode Island supporters were also arrested and punished. Legend has it that Kidd buried some of his treasure on Block Island. But no treasure has ever been found.

Slavery in Rhode Island

One of Rhode Island's most valuable businesses was also its most terrible. Rhode Island, especially Newport, became one of the top places in the colonies for buying and selling slaves. After King Philip's War, Newport ships carried Narragansett, Wampanoag, and other native people to the West Indies to be sold into slavery. In 1696, the first shipload of slaves from Africa was brought into the colony and sold. In time, Newport became the top slaving port in the world. Much of the town's money came from this trade.

Escaped slaves had to run for their lives from slave hunters.

The business of bringing slaves to the colonies from Africa was known as the "triangular trade." Rhode Island was one corner of the triangle. Here, molasses from the West Indies was made into rum at one of the colony's thirty rum factories, called distilleries. Newport alone was home to twenty-two rum distilleries. The rum was then shipped to Africa and used to buy slaves.

Africa was another corner of the triangle. Next, the slaves were shipped to the West Indies, the third corner of the triangle. There the slaves were exchanged for more molasses as well as sugar and other goods. Finally, these goods were shipped back to Newport. Some slaves were also brought back to Rhode Island, to be sold to settlers in the South as well as in nearby colonies. During the mid-1700s, Africans were sold for about $175 each at Newport slave markets. In today's money, this would be more than $4,000.

Stopping the Slave Trade

In 1774, Rhode Island stopped the importing of slaves into the colony. The General Assembly declared:

"The inhabitants of America are generally engaged in the preservation of their own rights and liberties, among which that of personal freedom must be considered the greatest, and...those who are desirous of enjoying all the advantage of liberty themselves should be willing to extend personal liberty to others." The General Assembly was saying, in other words, that people in America wanted freedom for themselves. They now realized that it was not fair to take away the freedom of others by forcing them into slavery.

The Voyage to America

The trip the slaves were forced to take from Africa to the West Indies was called the Middle Passage. It was infamous for its horrifying conditions. The voyage took about two months. The slaves were treated like animals. In the bottom of the ship, Africans were chained together side by side on wooden bunks. Sometimes they were packed so tightly that they had to be chained lying on their sides, with the head of one slave touching the toes of another.

Slaves were usually given gruel (a thin porridge) to eat once a day. Sometimes they were allowed to go outside on the ship's deck if the weather was good. Vomit, feces, and other body fluids were rinsed off the slaves once every two weeks. These dirty conditions were dangerous. On most voyages, more than one-fourth of the slaves died during the Middle Passage. The sick and dying were dumped into the sea so as not to slow down the voyage. On one voyage, 109 of the 167 slaves died before they reached the colonies.

Over the years, Rhode Island merchants sponsored at least 934 voyages to Africa to buy slaves. Some historians believe that more than 100,000 Africans came to America aboard Rhode Island slave ships. The slave trade in Rhode Island slowed after 1774. That year, Rhode Island passed a law banning the bringing of slaves into the colony. The law, however, did not free the slaves already there.

The Middle Passage

In an autobiography written in 1789, former African slave Olaudah Equiano described how some of his fellow captives were affected by the voyage from Africa to Barbados, in the West Indies:

Slaves were packed so close together aboard slave ships that they could hardly move.

"One day, when we had a smooth sea and a moderate wind, two of my wearied countrymen, who were chained together...preferring death to such a life of misery, somehow made it through the nettings and jumped into the sea; immediately another quite dejected fellow, who on account of his illness was suffered to be out of irons also followed their example; and I believe many more would very soon have done the same, if they had not been prevented by the ship's crew, who were instantly alarmed. Those of us who were the most active were in a moment put down under the deck; and there was such a noise and confusion amongst the people of the ship as I have never heard before, to stop her and get the boat out to go after the slaves. However, two of the wretches were drowned; but they got the other, and afterward flogged [whipped] him unmercifully, for thus attempting to prefer death to slavery."

Wealthy Merchants

Because of the trade in slaves and goods, Newport grew and prospered. Soon, there was an upper class made up of wealthy merchants. Rich people in Newport had a very different lifestyle than other colonists did. With their riches, the merchants built big, beautiful homes and filled them with expensive furniture imported from Europe and other places. These Newport mansions were usually two or three stories and often had a large room for entertaining guests.

Wealthy Newport residents were also known for being fashionable. Most other Rhode Islanders wore plain, practical clothing. Newport's rich wore stylish and colorful clothing. Ladies' dresses were trimmed with lace. The high-heeled shoes worn by both men and women had silver or gold buckles. Their accessories included powdered wigs, fans, and jeweled swords.

The wealthy people of Newport also used their money to improve their town. They paid to have the ports and streets cleaned up. They started libraries and supported artists and fine craftsmen. Newport was a wonderful place to be for the rich. It soon began attracting wealthy people from the southern colonies. Many wealthy colonists from Georgia, South Carolina, and Maryland bought or rented summer homes in Newport. In their summer homes, the families held balls and dinners for wealthy guests.

Rich Newport merchants dressed in their finest clothes to attend parties with music and dancing.

Wealthy Farmers

Although shipping dominated Rhode Island's economy, farming was still big business in the part of the colony known as Narragansett country. Located south of Providence, the Narragansett country was famous for its fertile soil. No other place in the region was better for farming.

There was a small group of wealthy landowners in the area known as the Narragansett Planters. The planters owned large farms called plantations of up to 7,000 acres (2,800 hectares) in size (about the size of the whole town of Newport). They mainly produced cattle and dairy products, sheep, horses, and pigs. One dairy product, Narragansett cheese, was loved by people throughout the colonies and in England as well. Narragansett cheese was made with milk and cream. It was famous for its rich, strong flavor.

Narragansett country was located in the perfect place to export its goods. It was close enough to the western shore of Narragansett Bay to make shipping possible. The planters made this even easier by digging a canal between the shore and Point Judith Pond, a large saltwater pond more than 2.5 square miles (6.5 square kilometers) in size. At the pond, small boats were packed full of goods and livestock from the plantations. The boats then sailed to the piers the planters had built on Narragansett Bay. Most of the cargo was then sent to Newport, the main shipping port in the colony.

Many Rhode Island farmers raised dairy cattle. Children were often responsible for herding the cattle back to the barn for milking.

Slaves did the work on the plantations of Narragansett country. Most of these slaves were African, but some were Native American. The number of slaves on each plantation varied, from five on smaller farms to as many as forty on larger ones. Slaves lived in the attic or in a separate wing of a planter's home. Between 1700 and 1750, the number of slaves working the Narragansett plantations grew quickly as the region prospered. The area had more slaves than any of the surrounding colonies.

The planter's mansion was the most impressive sight on each plantation. These large homes were furnished with goods imported from Europe and from other colonies. Although they weren't as fancy as the houses of Newport's wealthy, Narragansett plantation homes were big and comfortable.

Social events were often related to farming. Corn-husking festivals, called husking bees, for example, were eagerly awaited autumn events. At a husking bee, people who had traveled to the plantation from around the region helped to husk (remove the outer covering from) the host's corn. A feast and dance followed the work.

In the early 1700s, the lives of many colonists throughout Rhode Island were better than they had ever been before. But events in England and at home would soon threaten their well-being. Rhode Islanders would have to come together again to defend their way of life.

The Narragansett Pacer

On the Narragansett plantations, farmers needed strong horses to plow their fields. Legend has it that one farmer, Rowland Robinson, developed the perfect animal for the job. It was a horse he called the Narragansett Pacer. Robinson bred Arabian horses with native horses to develop a big, heavy horse capable of carrying huge loads. Despite its size, however, the animal was still able to move swiftly.

Throughout the 1700s, demand for Narragansett Pacers skyrocketed. Sales of the horses added to the wealth of the plantation owners. George Washington was thought to own two Narragansett Pacers, which he bought for racing. The horse was also popular in the West Indies because it didn't mind the hot tropical temperatures there.

By 1800, plantation owners had sold all of the Narragansett Pacers that there were in Rhode Island. The demand for them slowed. Farmers no longer bred the animals so there would be more. People elsewhere also stopped breeding the horses, and the Narragansett Pacer quickly became extinct.

Colonial craftsmen (artisans) made most of the things colonists needed. Craftsmen used simple tools to fashion everything from silver cups to wagon wheels by hand.

This carpenter's plane was used to shave and level wood. The blade could be adjusted to cut the wood at different depths.

A chisel such as this was used to shape wooden objects. The craftsman struck it with a wooden mallet or hammer to shape wood.

A compass made drawing a circle easy. It also was used to measure objects.

This handcrafted wooden box once held a craftsman's tools.

The shape and design of the handsaw has not changed much since colonial times.

70

Tools

☙ Tongs were used like pliers to hold objects while the artisan worked on them.

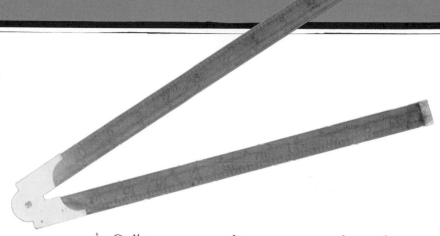

🜨 Calipers were used to measure angles and to draw plans.

☙ This silver-smith is hammering a silver cup into shape. Silversmiths were among the most skilled colonial craftsmen.

✍ An awl was used to punch holes in wood or leather.

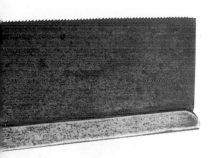

☞ Even wagon wheels had to be made by hand. The wheel-wright was a skilled craftsman who built each wheel from wood. Then he wrapped the wheel's edge with a metal rim.

CHAPTER FIVE

Uniting Behind a Cause

The Dominion of New England

Ten years after King Philip's War ended, trouble with Great Britain began. In 1685, James II became king. James wanted to tighten his control over the American colonies. In 1686 he declared that Connecticut, Massachusetts, New Hampshire, New Jersey, New York, and Rhode Island would now be one colony, called the Dominion of New England. To control the new colony, James made Sir Edmund Andros its governor.

Andros took control of Rhode Island's government in December 1686. He became the most hated man in the colony when he demanded Rhode Island's charter and broke the colony's **seal**. The seal was a special stamp used to mark

☙ *Edmund Andros moved the capital of the Dominion of New England to Boston but was soon arrested and sent back to England.*

official documents from Rhode Island's government. Without the seal, no documents the government made up would be legal.

In late 1688, James II was overthrown in Great Britain and was no longer king. When Massachusetts officials heard the news, they arrested Governor Andros. He was sent back to England in 1690. Rhode Island quickly returned to its original government, with an elected governor.

Prosperous Times

After Andros left, things went smoothly between Great Britain and the colonies for many years. During the early 1700s, Rhode Island continued to prosper. Under Governor Samuel Cranston, the colony was stronger and more united than ever before. Cranston also worked hard to create a better relationship with Great Britain.

In the early eighteenth century, Rhode Island grew in both size and population. Between 1726 and 1747, the colony added Cumberland, Bristol, and other towns on the eastern side of Narragansett Bay. Before this, these towns were claimed by both Connecticut and Massachusetts. As a result, Rhode Island's population in 1774 totaled more than 59,700 colonists in twenty-nine towns.

Newport was still the colony's most important economic and cultural center. But chocolate was coming to Providence.

The city of Providence grew and prospered during the mid-1700s.

Making Chocolate

The Brown family had arrived in Rhode Island in 1638. By the mid-1700s, four Brown brothers, Nicholas, Joseph, John, and Moses, controlled businesses in Providence and other Rhode Island towns. Their company's name was Nicholas Brown and Brothers. The brothers got wealthy through shipbuilding, trading, and privateering.

One of the Brown brothers' most unusual businesses was making chocolate. In 1739, Obadiah Brown, an uncle of the four brothers, founded Rhode Island's first chocolate mill. At the mill, cocoa beans were ground to make chocolate. Rhode Island soon became known as the chocolate capital of the colonies. When Obadiah died, the chocolate business went to his nephews, the Brown brothers.

With help from the Brown family, Providence began to challenge Newport as the most important town in the colony. The Brown brothers gave money to start schools and churches. They held dances and dinner parties at their mansions. The huge, fancy homes of the Browns were some of the most beautiful in the region. In 1789, a future president of the United States, John Quincy Adams visited John Brown's home. Adams described it as the most "magnificent and elegant" mansion he had seen in the country.

Communicating in the Colonies

In early colonial times, packet boats were used to deliver letters, packages, and passengers from one colony to another. A packet boat was a small vessel with sails. Depending upon the wind and the weather, a trip from Rhode Island to New York City on a packet boat might take anywhere from eighteen hours to a week.

In the early 1700s, a colonial postal system was begun. By 1707, there was a weekly mail delivery between Boston and many colonies, including Rhode Island. This mail was carried by messengers on horseback. Bad weather and roads often made delivery difficult. A letter might take up to six weeks to arrive at its destination.

Colonial post riders announced the arrival of the mail by blowing a horn.

Education, Arts, and Culture

Politics often took center stage during the early and mid-1700s, but Rhode Islanders also found time for education, arts, and culture. In 1729, writer Dean Berkeley arrived in Newport. While living in Rhode Island, he wrote a number of well-known poems. Another Rhode Island poet who was famous during this period was John Maylem. Maylem wrote poems about warfare and battles between colonists, native peoples, and the French.

Education was important during this time. Rhode Island College was founded in 1764 in Warren. Later, the college was renamed Brown University when one of the Brown brothers, Nicholas, left the school a large amount of money. In 1750, the first lending library in America was opened in Newport.

Although Rhode Islanders supported literature and art, they did not feel the same about theater. Like surrounding colonies, Rhode Island frowned on music and theater, mostly for religious reasons. Not until the mid-1700s did Newport residents begin enjoying plays and musical concerts.

In 1762, a theater company from London, England, came to Providence to perform. They brought new entertainment. At a town meeting, some residents voted to cancel the show. Others disagreed, and the play went on as planned.

America's first lending library opened in Newport, making books more available to Rhode Island's colonists.

To protect the actors, one Rhode Island resident guarded the door with a cannon. The following month, however, Rhode Island banned theater performances. The ban would remain in place for more than twenty years.

British Taxes

The early 1700s were years of prosperity. But problems between the colonies and the British motherland were growing worse. Great Britain began passing new laws that harmed Rhode Island's economy. These laws restricted trade in the colonies. The laws also placed large taxes on goods that came to America from anywhere but Britain and its other colonies.

In 1733, Great Britain passed the Molasses Act. This act put a heavy tax on imported molasses, sugar, and rum. All of these items were a major part of Rhode Island's triangular trade. As a result, many colonial merchants became upset and angry. Some began sneaking molasses into Rhode Island from non-British sources.

More Taxes

In the 1760s, Great Britain passed even harsher laws. Under these laws, goods such as sugar, newspapers, and printed materials were taxed. To make sure that colonists obeyed the new laws, British officers began checking the cargoes of boats going into and coming out of Rhode Island ports.

The colonists were furious. They did not think that they should have to pay taxes to England when there was no one in Great Britain's **Parliament** to represent the colonies and defend their rights. The rallying cry throughout the colonies became "No taxation without representation!"

In October 1765, Rhode Island took part in the Stamp Act Congress. The congress was created to issue an official protest to the mother country about another new law, the Stamp Act. This law required colonists to buy special government stamps for all printed material. The stamps were a kind of tax.

Rhode Island governor Samuel Ward decided to take his colony's protests a step farther. He refused to punish Rhode Islanders who didn't obey the Stamp Act. By May 1766, Great Britain **repealed,** or ended, the act.

This victory for the colonies was a small one. Great Britain continued to pass laws that taxed colonial goods. The new laws placed taxes on glass, lead, dye, paper, and tea imported into the colonies. The laws also tightened British control over the colonies and their governments.

The authors of the Stamp Act carry the law to its grave in this eighteenth-century cartoon. It was published shortly after the Stamp Act was repealed in 1766.

Kidnapping at Sea

Another issue that caused problems between Rhode Island and Great Britain was **impressment**. Impressment was the British practice of kidnapping men in Newport and other port cities and forcing them to work on British ships. In 1765, Rhode Island's disgust with the practice boiled over into violence. That year, about 500 Newport residents captured a small boat belonging to the British ship *Maidstone* and burned it. They also took one of the ship's officers captive. They were stopped, however, before they seriously harmed the man.

Rhode Island was a small colony that supported itself through shipping and trading. The British taxes threatened the colony's booming economy. Rhode Islanders had also become used to controlling their own government. The colony had been allowed self-government almost since its founding. Rhode Islanders were not about to give up any of their freedoms without a fight.

Most of Rhode Island's residents were united in their anger at Great Britain. Merchants, farmers, and tradesmen alike began to feel that it was time to cut the strings that tied the colonies to the motherland. Perhaps more than any other colony, Rhode Island was prepared for revolution.

Acts of Rebellion

Some Rhode Islanders had already begun to take part in acts of rebellion against Great Britain. The first such act took place in 1764. On July 9, the British ship *St. John* seized a colonial cargo of sugar. Newport residents were furious.

Colonists met in small groups called the Sons of Liberty to protest British treatment of the colonists before the American Revolution.

They began throwing stones at the boat. Later, some residents captured Fort George. The fort, built by Rhode Island to protect Narragansett Harbor, was manned by British troops. After taking the fort, the Newport residents fired its cannon at the *St. John*.

In 1769, when the British ship *Liberty* towed a captured Connecticut ship into Newport harbor, Newport's residents again took action. That night, they cut the cables that tied the *Liberty*. When the ship drifted ashore, the colonists burned it. The same year, Providence residents kidnapped a tax collector, beat him, then tarred and feathered him. (Tarring and feathering was a harsh colonial punishment. Hot tar was first poured over a person's body, which was then covered with feathers.)

As problems between colonists and the British grew, **Sons of Liberty** groups sprang up throughout Rhode Island. The first Sons of Liberty group had been organized by Boston merchants and tradesmen in 1765 to oppose the Stamp Act. As more groups were formed throughout the colonies, they began working together to create a united response to Great Britain.

Liberty Trees were also found in Providence, Newport, and other Rhode Island towns. Liberty Trees were meeting spots where people talked about the problems with Great Britain. Providence's Liberty Tree was dedicated in July

1768 by Patriot Silas Downer. At the dedication, Downer said, "May [the tree] long flourish."

When news of the problems in Rhode Island got back to Great Britain, King George III took action. He sent more ships and troops into Newport to keep the colonists under control. This only made the colonists more determined than ever to resist the British.

The Burning of the *Gaspee*

Rhode Island's boldest act of rebellion yet against Great Britain occurred in 1772. In March of that year, the British ship *Gaspee* arrived in Newport. The *Gaspee*'s mission was to end colonial smuggling. Throughout the spring, the captain and crew of the *Gaspee* stopped and inspected colonial ships leaving Newport.

On June 9, 1772, the *Hannah,* a colonial trading ship, refused to stop for the *Gaspee*. The British ship chased after the *Hannah*, but the *Gaspee*'s captain and crew were not familiar with the coastal waters. The chase ended when the *Gaspee* became stuck on a sandbar near Warwick.

When the *Hannah* arrived in Providence, its captain told local merchants about the stranded British ship. The city's Patriots saw their chance to get back at Great Britain. That night, a group of Rhode Islanders, led by John Brown, Joseph Brown, and Abraham Whipple, rowed out to the

Angry Rhode Island colonists burned the British ship Gaspee *in Providence harbor before the start of the American Revolution.*

Gaspee. They captured the ship's captain and crew. Then they set the ship on fire. The act was declared "high treason" by King George, and British officials offered a large reward for the names of those responsible. However, no one was ever turned in or punished. This showed that most Rhode Island colonists did not support the British.

Fanning the Flames

Rhode Islanders knew that the problems with Great Britain might lead to war and bloodshed. In December 1774, the colony removed all the cannons, guns, and gunpowder from Fort George. Captain James Wallace of the British warship *Rose* asked Rhode Island's governor why the weapons had been removed. In a report, Wallace recorded the governor's answer: "He very frankly told me they had done it to prevent [the weapons] falling into the hands of the King or any of his servants; and that they meant to make use of them to defend themselves against any power that shall offer to [bother] them."

Standing Up to the British

After helping to burn the *Gaspee*, Abraham Whipple received a note from Sir James Wallace, commander of the British ship *Rose:*

"You, Abraham Whipple, on the 10th June, 1772, burned His Majesty's vessel, the *Gaspee*, and I will hang you to the yard arm."

To which Whipple replied:

"*Sir,* always catch a man before you hang him."

Wallace never did manage to capture Whipple, who went on to serve as commodore of the U.S. Navy during the American Revolution. Whipple died in Ohio in 1809, at the age of 85.

Anger against the British was fanned by the colony's newspapers. Both Newport's *Rhode Island Gazette* and the *Providence Gazette and Country Journal* played a major role in adding fuel to the fire. In 1768, for example, Newport's *Gazette* ran an article called "Join or Die." The article encouraged the colonies to join together against the mother country. Pamphlets calling for rebellion and revolution were also published in Rhode Island's two main towns.

Another act of rebellion occurred on March 2, 1775. As a protest against the tax on tea, all of Providence's residents were invited to a public bonfire. Town officials urged citizens to bring the "needless herb" to Market Square in the center of town. People piled their tea into a huge heap. Then they poured tar over it and lit it on fire. Tea was taken out of all town stores, and no good patriot would drink it.

Declaring Freedom

On April 19, 1775, British soldiers and American Patriots battled at Lexington and Concord in Massachusetts. Many Rhode Islanders wanted to march to Massachusetts to fight, but Governor Joseph Wanton refused to allow it. Rhode Islanders were furious. As a result, Wanton was suspended and, six months later, forced out of office as governor.

Rhode Island's militia prepared for war as the colony's representatives to the Second Continental Congress met in Philadelphia.

On May 4, 1776, Rhode Island became the first colony to declare its independence from Great Britain. The General Assembly passed the Independence Act two months before the rest of the colonies declared their freedom on July 4, 1776. The Independence Act accused King George III of "forgetting his dignity" and "departing from the duties and Character of a good King."

In June 1776, Stephen Hopkins, former governor of Rhode Island, and William Ellery, a Newport lawyer, traveled to Philadelphia, Pennsylvania, to represent Rhode Island at the Second Continental Congress. The Second Continental Congress was a meeting of colonial representatives to determine what actions should be taken against England. On July 4, Hopkins and Ellery approved the Declaration of Independence, which they signed in early August on behalf of Rhode Island's colonists. The document officially ended the thirteen colonies' relationship with Great Britain and created the United States of America.

After the Declaration, most colonies began making state constitutions to spell out rules and regulations. Rhode Island's General Assembly decided that, with some changes, the charter that had existed since 1663 would work just fine. In fact, the charter would be used to guide Rhode Island's government for another sixty-seven years.

CHAPTER SIX

The Fight for Freedom

Rhode Island Patriots

Rhode Island supported the struggle for independence before and during the Revolutionary War. Many great Revolutionary Patriots were born and raised in Rhode Island. Throughout the war, the colony contributed soldiers, weapons, and other supplies to the American cause.

One of the most famous and able of all of Rhode Island's Patriots was Nathanael Greene, from Warwick. In April 1775, Greene was made the commander of a 1,500-man fighting force. He and his troops fought in the Battle of Princeton in New Jersey, and in the Battles of Brandywine and Germantown in Pennsylvania. In 1780, Greene was put in charge of the southern revolutionary

ᗊ *General Nathanael Greene was Rhode Island's greatest Revolutionary War hero.*

army. That command made him second only to General George Washington.

Greene's successes in the southern colonies seriously weakened British control in the area. To thank him, Georgia, North Carolina, and South Carolina gave Greene land and other gifts. After the war, Greene retired in Georgia.

Life During the War

Many of Rhode Island's coastal towns suffered greatly during the war. Newport was especially hard-hit. Beginning in June 1775, a British **blockade** of the port caused Newport residents serious problems. During the blockade, British ships stopped food supplies from entering the port. The city

Doing His Part

One of the most unusual protests against the British happened in Newport early in the war. As a British ship sat in the harbor, a man named Coggeshall wandered out onto a wharf and "turned up his backsides towards the bomb-brig [ship]." He also yelled insults at the British crew. The crew responded by firing two shots at him. Although unhurt, Coggeshall was sent out of town by fellow residents who didn't think much of his odd display.

was also bombed by British warships. Soon, many Newport residents packed up their belongings and left the city.

From the coast of Newport, British soldiers raided area farms. They stole hay, food, and animals. These supplies were then sent to British troops in Boston. Many other towns, including Warren, Bristol, Portsmouth, Kingstown, and Greenwich, were also fired at from the water.

Providence was in a much safer location than other towns. It did not suffer the same problems. The town quickly became the main meeting place for the colony's Patriots. In Providence, guns and supplies were gathered to aid the Continental army. The Continental army had been organized by the Second Continental Congress in 1775. It was the first U.S. army.

Providence citizens pitched in to support the war effort. A schoolhouse was turned into a laboratory to make explosives. A building called Whipple Hall was made into a place to store gunpowder. It also served as a meeting place for Patriots. Later in the war, American and French troops stayed at Rhode Island College, which later became Brown University, and camped on the outskirts of the town.

Those who couldn't fight the British on the battlefield also did their part. Women held spinning bees to make their own fabric and cloth, so they wouldn't have to buy fabric imported from England. Others formed Daughters of Liberty groups to aid the fight for independence.

Colonial women spun their own thread and wove cloth to make their family's clothing in order to avoid buying British goods.

Newport Captured

In late 1776, times were tough for the Newport Patriots who had stayed in the city. On December 8, as many as 9,000 British and Hessian troops under Sir Henry Clinton took control of Newport. (Hessians were German soldiers hired to fight for the British.) Since Newport was one of the five most important colonial seaports, this was an important victory for the British.

For nearly three years, the British occupied, or stayed in, the town. During their stay, they destroyed orchards, fields, and public buildings, including the town's schoolhouse. Nearly 500 houses were burned.

In the winter, Newport residents were forced to provide shelter for British soldiers. The Colony House, Rhode Island's government building, was turned into a hospital. Most of the churches were turned into stables or housing for soldiers. The city's wharves were also destroyed.

The only residents safe from the destruction were town citizens who had stayed loyal to the king. These residents were called **Loyalists**, or **Tories**. Newport had a large number of Loyalists. During the occupation, Newport's Loyalists gave dinner parties for British military officers. The town even had three regiments of Loyalist soldiers who fought for the British. These were the Prince of Wales

Volunteers, the King's American Regiment, and the Loyal New Englanders.

From Newport, the British and their allies raided and burned neighboring towns. They captured town leaders and others who supported the rebel cause. After one raid, Fleet Green, a Newport resident on the side of the rebels, wrote: "The prisoners were all sent on board the Prison ships. This expedition has caused universal joy among the Tories."

Dealing With Loyalists in Rhode Island

Loyalists could be found in other Rhode Island towns besides Newport. While Newport's Loyalists were safe while the town was occupied by the British, Loyalists in other Rhode Island towns had to beware. Being loyal to the British or helping them in any way could be dangerous. The General Assembly often asked citizens who were suspected of knowing Loyalists to report them. The citizens usually obeyed the General Assembly.

Some Tories were hanged and burned in effigy. This means that dummies of Loyalists were hanged and burned instead of the actual people. A Loyalist shop owner in Providence awoke one morning to find that the front of his shop had been completely covered with tar and feathers.

Loyalists were often attacked by Patriots. This Tory is being strung up by his neighbors.

Rhode Island officials were anxious to get Newport back from the British. They first tried in August 1778 in a conflict called the Battle of Rhode Island. Although the Patriots lost the battle, it gave the colony's soldiers a chance to show their bravery and daring.

Black Troops and the Battle of Rhode Island

In 1778, the Continental Congress told Rhode Island that it must gather enough men for the Continental army to fill two battalions (a battalion consists of about 1,000 soldiers). Rhode Island turned to its black population to carry out this order.

Since Rhode Island was important in the slave trade, the population of blacks in the colony was higher than in any other nearby colony. In 1755, nearly 12 percent of the colony's people were black. Most of Rhode Island's black residents were slaves.

To fulfill the order from the Continental Congress, the General Assembly stated that "every able-bodied Negro, Mulatto or Indian Man slave, in this State, may enlist." Those who enlisted, or joined the army, were given their freedom along with soldier's pay. Slave owners whose slaves went into the army would be paid by the government.

Slave owners were not happy. They were worried that they wouldn't get the money they had been promised by the General Assembly. They may also have been worried about giving weapons to the men they had once owned. As a result, Rhode Island's new law was repealed within four months.

Even so, as many as 250 African-Americans signed up to serve in the First Rhode Island Regiment of the

Troops from Rhode Island fought for the Patriot army in many Revolutionary War battles.

Continental army, an all-black regiment. The regiment's commander, Colonel Christopher Greene, was happy to have them.

In August 1778, the First Rhode Island took part in the Battle of Rhode Island. During the battle, black soldiers fought side by side with white soldiers. Their goal was to drive the British out of Newport, but they were not successful.

The First Rhode Island continued to fight bravely throughout the rest of the war. Its members took part in battles at Red Bank, New Jersey; Yorktown, Virginia; and Fort Oswego and Points Bridge, New York. They left the army in June 1783, but they never got the pay they had been promised by the government.

The Bravery of the First Rhode Island

After the Battle of Rhode Island, a white soldier remembered the bravery of the First Rhode Island Regiment:

"There was a black regiment in the same situation. Yes, a regiment of negroes, fighting for our liberty and independence,—not a white man among them but the officers,—stationed in the same dangerous and responsible position. Had they been unfaithful or given way before the enemy, all would have been lost. Three times in succession were they attacked, with most desperate valor and fury, by well disciplined and veteran troops, and three times did they successfully repel the assault and thus preserve our army from capture."

A Victorious Ending

In the end, it did not take a battle to get the British to leave Newport. On October 25, 1779, the last British troops sailed out of Rhode Island. The soldiers had been ordered to report to New York. Once the British ships were on their way, Newport's remaining Patriots raced down to the shore and jeered at the departing troops.

The British left Newport nearly in ruins. One-third of Newport's population was gone. Many of the city's businesses were destroyed. The British also stole town records, books from one of Newport's libraries, and church bells.

With the British gone, the angry colonists moved quickly. They took control of property owned by Loyalists. They rebuilt forts and other town buildings that had been destroyed. George Washington even visited the ruined town to plan strategy with another general. He was honored with a grand party.

The war had dealt Newport a serious economic blow. It would take decades for the city to recover. In fact, Newport would never again be Rhode Island's business center. Many of Newport's tradesmen, workers, and merchants moved to Providence to continue their businesses. Soon, Providence would play an important role in forming the new nation for which Rhode Islanders had helped fight.

CHAPTER SEVEN
Statehood

Becoming American

After the war, being independent from Great Britain was not as hard for Rhode Island as it was for some other colonies. Rhode Islanders were used to governing themselves. Rhode Island had always had the most democratic government in the colonies. The colony's charter was still a good guide for its officials.

Like other colonies, however, Rhode Island had to work hard to recover after the war. Everywhere, people faced a period of economic hard times, known as a **depression.** Rhode Island's population dropped from about 58,000 before the war to 52,000 afterward.

Newport in particular faced many struggles. Like other coastal towns, it had been badly damaged by British raids and bombings. At first, the seaport turned back to slave

⚐ *When the Revolutionary War ended, many Loyalists were forced to leave the new state. They often left their homes, businesses, and belongings behind.*

trading to help its economy. Rhode Island's slave traders were not in business for very long, however. In 1784, Rhode Island's General Assembly passed a law freeing some of the state's slaves. The law stated, "All men are entitled to life, liberty, and property." All children born to slave mothers after March 1, 1784, were freed. The law did not emancipate, or free, all of the slaves, but it was a step in the right direction. In 1787, Rhode Island citizens were banned from taking part in the slave trade.

Unlike Newport, Providence prospered after the war. Rhode Island's first settlement now took Newport's place as the colony's business center. After the war, Providence's harbor was made deeper. This allowed larger ships to sail into the city, and trade skyrocketed. By 1814, more than one hundred vessels made Providence's port their home. Providence was changing from a town into an important New England city.

As Providence grew in importance, its merchants grew more powerful. Soon, Providence merchants refused to accept paper money as payment for goods. They said that the money was worthless and demanded gold or silver. In response, people in small farming communities held a farm strike. They burned their crops and poured out their milk to protest their lack of power. In the coming years, farming would decline in Rhode Island. Many people moved out of the small country towns and into Providence and other cities.

As business prospered in Providence, sailing ships lined the busy wharf. They carried goods of all kinds to and from Rhode Island as trade with the other states and Europe grew after the Revolutionary War.

Holding On to Independence

During the Revolution, many people talked about creating a strong government that would oversee all of the colonies. But many other Americans, including Rhode Islanders, did not trust a strong federal government. They were afraid that a powerful government would be as unfair to them as the British government had been. They feared that a new government would make people pay taxes that would hurt the individual states. Rhode Islanders, especially, did not want to give up the freedoms that their fellow colonists had fought and died for during the Revolution.

Because of this fear, Rhode Island decided not to send delegates (representatives) to the Constitutional Convention, which was held in 1787 in Philadelphia. Delegates from each colony were invited to this convention. Its purpose was to plan a new, strong federal government to unite the colonies. It was here that the U.S. Constitution was written, establishing the government of the United States.

After the finished Constitution was given to the states to ratify (approve), many people in Rhode Island spoke out against it. Even so, there were plenty of Rhode Islanders who wanted to approve the Constitution. Much dicussion took place. From 1787 to 1790, a number of politicians tried to form a state convention to ratify the Constitution.

The Constitutional Convention met in Independence Hall in Philadelphia in 1787. Delegates from Rhode Island did not attend.

Rhode Island leaders finally decided to let the people of Rhode Island vote whether they would ratify the Constitution. The result was 2,708 votes to 237 against ratifying the document. By rejecting the Constitution, Rhode Islanders had shown that they still did not trust a federal government.

First in War, Last in Peace

Many groups continued to fight for the U.S. Constitution. Rhode Island's merchants were one such group. They believed that a strong federal government would be better at handling money and improving Rhode Island's economy than Rhode Island's current government.

Many coastal towns also supported the new government. They wanted to be paid for the damage caused by the war. A federal government would have more money to do so.

Some people who opposed the Constitution changed their minds when the Bill of Rights was added to it. The Bill of Rights guaranteed that the fiercely independent Rhode Islanders would not have to give up all their rights to the federal government. But even with the Bill of Rights, many people still refused to let their state sign the document.

To get Rhode Island to sign, President George Washington and other federal officials promised that the new federal government would pay any money the states

The Bill of Rights, the first ten amendments added to the Constitution, guaranteed many individual rights. Its addition to the Constitution persuaded a majority in Rhode Island to join the new nation.

owed to others. Then they threatened Rhode Island with a tax for not joining the United States. They also demanded that all debts that Rhode Island owed to the new nation be repaid immediately. The final push to ratify the Constitution came from Providence, Rhode Island's most important town. Providence officials threatened that their city would break away from Rhode Island if the Constitution was not signed.

In January 1790, representatives at a constitutional convention in Rhode Island finally voted to ratify the Constitution. The vote was the closest of any state: 34 in favor of ratification, 32 against. On May 29, 1790, Rhode Island became the last of the original thirteen colonies to ratify the Constitution.

Into the Future

Even after signing the Constitution, Rhode Islanders continued to guard their independence and free government. For example, the state would not allow Rhode Island soldiers to serve under federal officers or to serve outside the state. In 1814, Rhode Island officials also supported changes to the Constitution that further protected the states' rights.

Being part of the United States of America affected Rhode Island's economy. Money from shipping now went straight to the federal government, not to the state. One of the most serious economic difficulties arose in 1807 with

George Washington led the country through the Revolutionary War. As the first president, he helped persuade Rhode Island to ratify the Constitution.

President Thomas Jefferson's **embargo** of international trade. An embargo is a government order that bans certain ships from entering or leaving the country's ports. The embargo hurt Rhode Island shipping. Many citizens were angry with Jefferson and the federal government.

Manufacturing became Rhode Island's major industry as the new state moved into the nineteenth century.

However, manufacturing was quickly replacing shipping and other businesses as the most important industry in Rhode Island. During this period, called the Industrial Revolution, many factories were built. For the first time, most goods were being made by machine instead of by hand.

The Industrial Revolution had started in Great Britain in the early 1700s. It would eventually change the entire economy of the United States. The Industrial Revolution started in America in 1790 when Samuel Slater founded a cotton mill in Rhode Island. Slater's factory and others would soon give the small state the economic boost it needed. These businesses would also change the way people in Rhode Island lived their everyday lives.

Rhode Island, though the smallest state in the United States, had grown from a collection of scattered settlements founded by those seeking religious and other freedoms into an important industrial center. Though politics, rebellion, and war had transformed life in the state, Rhode Islanders had always kept their independent spirit.

Recipe

Johnnycakes

Rhode Island settlers learned to make many types of foods from the Narragansett and other Indians. One favorite dish was Johnnycakes. These cornmeal pancakes are delicious and easy to make. Just gather the ingredients and follow these steps.

1 cup cornmeal or johnnycake meal
1/2 teaspoon salt
1 teaspoon sugar
1 cup milk
1 cup water
Butter or margarine

1. Mix dry ingredients together in a bowl.

2. Add water and milk to bowl and mix until well blended.

3. Grease a hot frying pan with butter or margarine.

4. Pour about 1/2 cup of the mixture into frying pan.

5. Cook until the edges of the johnnycake turn brown (about five minutes). Flip the cake and cook for about five more minutes.

6. Remove the cake and repeat steps 1–5 with the rest of the batter.

7. Eat with butter, jam, or maple syrup.

This activity should be done with adult supervision.

Activity
Dame Schools

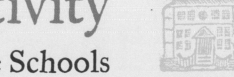

The first schools attended by many children living in the colonial era were called dame schools. The classes were taught by "dames," a name women often were called at that time. A dame school was located in a woman's home. The "dame" would work on her chores while students completed their schoolwork. Dame schools had no desks and hardly any books. There were no maps or chalkboards. The children learned simple lessons in reading and writing letters, numbers, and words.

Poems and riddles sometimes were used in math classes at dame schools to help students remember facts. Here are two examples of rhymes that could have been used in dame schools:

A gallon is made
Of quarts by the four.
How many quarts in a barrel
Nine gallons by the door?

A pentagon is drawn
With five different sides.
What's the sum of the angles
That inside it hides?

Write a riddle or poem to help a friend remember something you learned in math class. First, think about a subject, like measurements or shapes or fractions. Then write a poem. The first two lines in the examples provide the fact. The second two lines present a problem to solve. Try it!

RHODE ISLAND

Time Line

1524
Giovanni da Verrazano is the first European to explore Narragansett Bay.

1636
Roger Williams becomes first permanent settler in Rhode Island.

1639
Newport is settled on the southern tip of Aquidneck Island.

1647
Rhode Island's first General Assembly is formed.

1663
Great Britain grants a second charter to Rhode Island and the Providence Plantations that redraws the boundary between the colony and Connecticut.

1500   1525   1625   1650   1675

1614
Dutch trader Adriaen Block explores Rhode Island coast.

1616
Epidemic causes the deaths of hundreds of Wampanoag.

1638
Anne Hutchinson and others settle Portsmouth on Aquidneck Island.

1643
Rhode Island obtains first royal charter.

1675
King Philip's War causes the deaths of thousands of Native Americans and about 600 colonists.

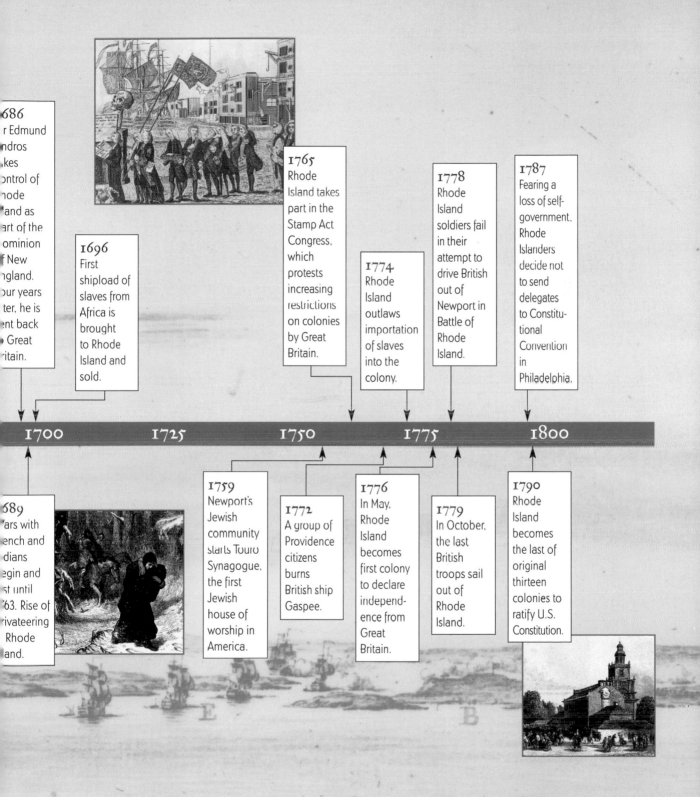

1686
[Si]r Edmund [A]ndros [ta]kes [c]ontrol of [R]hode [Isl]and as [p]art of the [D]ominion [of] New [E]ngland. [F]our years [la]ter, he is [s]ent back [to] Great [B]ritain.

1696
First shipload of slaves from Africa is brought to Rhode Island and sold.

1765
Rhode Island takes part in the Stamp Act Congress, which protests increasing restrictions on colonies by Great Britain.

1774
Rhode Island outlaws importation of slaves into the colony.

1778
Rhode Island soldiers fail in their attempt to drive British out of Newport in Battle of Rhode Island.

1787
Fearing a loss of self-government, Rhode Islanders decide not to send delegates to Constitutional Convention in Philadelphia.

1700   **1725**   **1750**   **1775**   **1800**

1689
[W]ars with [Fr]ench and [In]dians [b]egin and [la]st until [17]63. Rise of [p]rivateering [in] Rhode [Is]land.

1759
Newport's Jewish community starts Touro Synagogue, the first Jewish house of worship in America.

1772
A group of Providence citizens burns British ship Gaspee.

1776
In May, Rhode Island becomes first colony to declare independence from Great Britain.

1779
In October, the last British troops sail out of Rhode Island.

1790
Rhode Island becomes the last of original thirteen colonies to ratify U.S. Constitution.

Further Reading

Allison, Amy. *Roger Williams: Founder of Rhode Island.* Philadelphia: Chelsea House, 2001.

Burgan, Michael. *Colonial and Revolutionary Times.* New York: Franklin Watts, 2003.

Sioux, Tracee. *Immigrants in Colonial America.* New York: PowerKids Press, 2004.

Thoennes Keller, Kristin. *The Slave Trade in Early America.* Mankato, MN: Capstone Press, 2004.

Walker, Niki. *Colonial Women.* New York: Crabtree, 2003.

Glossary

blockade the blocking of a port with ships to prevent food and other goods from entering or exiting

charter written document giving a colony permission to exist

depression period of hard economic times

embargo government order that bans certain ships from entering or leaving the country's ports

epidemic rapid spread of disease to a large number of people

impressment the act of kidnapping men to serve as sailors on ships

Liberty Tree meeting place where Patriots talked about the troubles with Great Britain

Loyalist person who remained loyal to Great Britain during the American Revolution. Also called a Tory.

Navigation Acts laws created by Great Britain in the late 1600s to protect British trade

nomad person who moves from place to place in search of food

Parliament Great Britain's lawmaking body

Patriot person who sided with the colonists fighting the British during the American Revolution.

privateer person who owned a ship hired by a government to attack and rob enemy ships

Quaker member of a religious group that followed a special set of rules and customs

repeal put an end to; set aside

sachem chief of a Native American tribe

seal stamp used to identify official government documents

Sons of Liberty secret groups of Patriots formed to protest British laws

tannery shop where animal skins are turned into leather

thatch roof covering made of straw or leaves

Tory person who remained loyal to Great Britain during the American Revolution. Also called a Loyalist.

wigwam the kind of home built by some Native American tribes

Index